EARTH'S CHANGING LANDSCAPE

Weather & Climate

John Corn

FRANKLIN WATTS
LONDON•SYDNEY

This edition 2007

Franklin Watts
338 Euston Road
London NW1 3BH

Franklin Watts Australia
Hachette Children's Books
Level 17/207 Kent Street
Sydney, NSW 2000

Series editor: Sarah Peutrill
Series designer: Simon Borrough
Art director: Jonathan Hair
Picture researchers: Juliet Duff and Diana Morris
Series consultant: Steve Watts, FRGS, Principal Lecturer in
Geography Education at the University of Sunderland

A CIP catalogue record for this book is available from the British
Library

ISBN: 978 0 7496 7266 9
Dewey Classification: 551.6

Printed in Malaysia

Picture credits:
Andrew Brown/Ecoscene: 9, 11, 32, 36, 37, 38. Christiana
Carvalho/FLPA: 18, 25. John Corbett/Ecoscene: 22. Eric
Crichton/Corbis: 7b. James Davis Worldwide: 8. Nigel Dickinson/Still
Pictures: 16b. Digital Vision: 14, 15t, 19, 30-31, 38 inset, 39, 42. Mark
Edwards/Still Pictures: 15b. David Hoadley/FLPA: front cover, 17.
Keystone Praha/Rex: 13. John Kieffer/Still Pictures: 28. Frans
Lanting/Minden/FLPA: 21. Brigitte Marcon/Still Pictures: 27. Sally
Morgan/Ecoscene: 10. NASA: 16t, 43. Fritz Polking/Ecoscene: 24.
Francois Savigny/Still Pictures: 7t. Erik Schaffer/Ecoscene: 40. Sipa/Rex:
12, 29. Paul Thompson/Eye Ubiquitous: 33. S. Tiwari/Ecoscene: 41. Brian
A. Vikander/Corbis: 35. W Wisniewski/FLPA: 26. Gunter Ziesler/Still
Pictures: 34.

Franklin Watts is a division of Hachette Children's Books.

CONTENTS

Weather refers to what is happening in the atmosphere at the moment. It is concerned with temperature, rainfall, wind speed, wind direction, sunshine and cloud. The weather can alter the landscape dramatically in a few hours through extreme phenomenon such as hurricanes, but it can also change it very slowly over time through weathering and erosion.

Ever changing Weather can change constantly. In a few minutes temperatures may rise or fall, the wind may increase or decrease in speed and change direction. Clouds may build up to obscure the Sun or clear away to reveal bright sunshine.

The atmosphere Weather is caused by the air that surrounds the planet, called the atmosphere, cooling down and warming up. The atmosphere is made up of five layers. Weather happens only in the layer that is nearest to the Earth.

The Sun The Sun is an important influence on the weather. The Sun's rays warm the Earth's surface and this then heats the air above it. The Earth moves slowly around the Sun once every year. Different places become closer to the Sun through the year and this gives us the different weather patterns we call seasons. In different climates (see pages 24-41) the weather bought about by the seasons has a major effect on the Earth's landscape.

Air pressure Air pressure – which is caused by gravity – also affects what the weather will be like. Low air pressure usually indicates cloudy, rainy weather. High air pressure usually indicates fine, clear weather.

This early morning mist has been caused by low pressure. The Sun's rays are less powerful as they have to shine through the mist to warm the Earth's surface.

Follow it through: the Sirocco

Hot dry air moves north from the Sahara

It meets cooler humid air over the Mediterranean

Clouds Clouds reduce the amount of energy reaching the Earth from the Sun during the day. They stop much of the warm air escaping at night, so acting like a 'cloud blanket'. Places that have a lot of cloud experience only small changes in their daytime and night time temperatures compared with places, such as deserts, where cloud cover is much less.

Wind Wind is caused by air in the Earth's atmosphere moving from one place to another. The air moves from areas of high pressure to low pressure. The pressure differences are caused by the Sun heating up the air. Warm air is lighter so it rises, creating low pressure. Cool air is heavier so it sinks and creates high pressure.

Wind can have both long-term and short-term effects on the landscape. Over a long time trees on windy hillsides grow more leaves on their sheltered sides, away from the wind. Winds can also be massively powerful and cause sudden destruction to a landscape.

With little cloud cover, this desert receives hot temperatures during the day and cold temperatures at night.

An English yew tree shaped by coastal winds.

Case study: the Sirocco

There are different types of wind depending on location, for example coastal winds and mountain-valley winds. There are also desert winds, such as the Sirocco.

The Sirocco is a southerly wind, which draws in hot air from a large area of the northern Sahara Desert normally in the spring and early summer. The air passes over the Mediterranean Sea, which is about 10°C cooler but far more humid. When these two air masses meet, heavy rain and thunderstorms develop and winds can reach over 50 kilometres per hour.

The resulting heavy storms may reach the European shores of the Mediterranean Sea, causing damage to crops. Local people often complain about headaches, depression and sleeping problems. The air contains large quantities of sand and dust, much of which comes down with the rain. This dust has been found as far north as the Netherlands.

Storms and heavy rain develop → Strong winds occur → There is damage to crops

WEATHERING

Many things, when they are left outside, begin to break down: metal rusts, wood cracks and even the stones on ancient buildings or gravestones show signs of decay. This is because they have been exposed to the weather.

What is weathering?

Weathering describes the processes through which rock and other materials are broken down by the weather. The process begins as soon as new material is exposed to the atmosphere. It will take several hundred years for lettering on gravestones to become unreadable. And over thousands or millions of years, weathering can have a dramatic effect on the landscape.

Physical weathering

'Frost wedging' occurs when water expands as it freezes, enlarging cracks in rocks and causing them over time to split. When this happens chunks of rock break away, and on steep valley sides they may accumulate to form 'scree'.

Rocks heated by the Sun expand during the day, but at night they cool and contract. This causes cracks to appear in their surface. Eventually layers of rock will 'peel off' and fall to the ground. These are called 'exfoliation domes'. This is a common process in desert areas that experience extremes of temperatures during the day.

Scree has formed on the sides of this mountain in Italy.

Follow it through: rock changes

Rocks heated by the Sun expand

Rocks cool at night and contract

Take it further

Find out about a limestone landscape using the Internet, for example see www.malhamdale.org.uk.

◆ Download some of the information and photographs you find and make a leaflet advertising the area and its scenery.
◆ Display these with maps and other tourist information that you can find.

Chemical weathering

Carbon dioxide, which is a gas contained in the air, dissolves in rainwater and makes it slightly acidic. This acid will over time react with minerals in rocks and either dissolve them or turn them into other minerals.

The features that are produced as a result of chemical weathering can be dramatic. In the Yorkshire Dales in the UK there are large areas of 'limestone pavement' – exposed limestone that is covered with deep gulleys created by rainwater. There are also 'swallow holes' – gaps in the limestone through which rivers may disappear into cave systems. Here, water slowly tricking through the limestone evaporates to leave deposits of calcium in the form of stalagmites and stalactites. Over time, the walls of an underground cave will enlarge so much that its roof will collapse to form a steep-sided gorge.

Over thousands of years, acidic rainwater has dissolved weak areas of the limestone to create deep cracks at Malham Cove, Yorkshire, UK

Rock becomes unstable → Rocks crack and peel → They form smaller rock fragments, sand and dust

EROSION

Athabasca Glacier in the Canadian Rocky Mountain National Park.

Erosion occurs when particles of rock and soil are loosened by weathering, or by physical means, and begin to move. This is usually due to the action of glaciers, wind or water. It is possible to find evidence of erosion in most landscapes, as it is responsible for the creation of hills, valleys, coasts and many more features.

Glaciation Glaciers and ice sheets cover about 10 per cent of the Earth's surface. Ice sheets are areas of seawater that are frozen to a great depth. They are mostly found in the polar regions. Smaller glaciers of compact ice and snow occur in high mountain ranges.

In the ice age (see page 22), ice sheets and mountain glaciers expanded to cover much of northern Europe and America and carved the landscape into the form we see today.

Follow it through: glaciers

Snow and ice accumulate in a corrie on a mountainside

Snow compacts into hard ice

Glacier formation

Glaciers are formed in armchair-like hollows known as 'corries', often thousands of metres up a mountain. Over hundreds of years, snow builds up in the hollows and, because of the cold and weight of snow, it gradually turns to ice. These huge blocks of ice are then drawn by gravity down the mountain valley. They erode at the sides and make the valley into a U-shape.

Rock fragments of all sizes are dragged along and they scour the land and remove huge quantities of soil, heaping it along the sides and front of the glacier as 'moraine'. In the summer glaciers melt a little, creating meltwater streams that flow down the mountainsides into the valleys below.

Wind Wind is an important agent of erosion. In places that are dry with loose soil, such as deserts, the wind picks up particles of dust and sand and uses them to sand-blast boulders into smooth-rounded shapes. Rock faces are often undercut because the particles of sand are carried into the air by only one or two metres.

Sand grains blown by the wind can form drifts or dunes in the shape of ridges and crescents, which slowly move in the direction of the wind.

An arch formed by wind erosion, Arches National Park, Utah, USA.

Water Rivers also cause erosion, particularly after heavy rain. Rivers carry weathered material, such as soil and stones, so that over time river valleys are made deeper and wider by erosion. As a river passes over rocks of different hardness, it erodes them at different speeds and this helps to produce a variety of landforms including rapids, gorges, waterfalls and meanders.

Hard ice eventually becomes so heavy it begins to move

The glacier erodes the valley sides, creating a U-shaped valley

Rock and soil, eroded from the valley, form moraines in front of the glacier

FLOODS

Floods are an extreme weather event, and occur for many reasons, but usually after a long spell of heavy rain, when rivers cannot cope with the volume of water. Evidence based on rising sea temperatures and average land temperatures suggests that floods will become more commonplace in the future.

Major impact

Floods can cause tremendous changes to the landscape, especially if they occur without warning. A few centimetres of water inside a house will ruin furnishings, plasterwork and decorations and damage the electricity supply. Fifty centimetres of fast-flowing water has the power to move cars, knock people down and sweep them away. Within a few minutes, floods can destroy bridges and buildings, roll cars and uproot trees.

Mudslides

Heavy rain falling in areas of high land or on steep ground can cause mudslides and landslips. When heavy rain soaks deep into the ground it loosens the rocks and soil beneath. Under the force of gravity the ground collapses and moves quickly down the slope, often taking trees and sometimes houses with it.

A mudslide in Italy, caused by heavy rain.

Coastal flooding

Floods can also occur when a storm sweeps across a coastline or when a hurricane reaches land. Flash floods – sudden, intense torrential rain – can also cause flooding.

One example of this, combined with coastal erosion, is of the Holbeck Hall Hotel in Scarborough, UK. Here trees that had been planted to hold the soil in place in front of the hotel had been removed so that guests could enjoy the view along the coast towards the town. As time passed the land became more and more unstable until one morning in 1993, after heavy rain, guests woke to find that the hotel was slowly collapsing into the sea.

Case study: European floods 2002

In August 2002 Central and Eastern Europe suffered widespread flooding after freak storms and prolonged heavy rainfall.

Prague

One of the first places to be swamped by the floodwater was Prague, in the Czech Republic. Here the River Vltava rose between 10 and 15 centimetres an hour to a total of 8 metres above its usual height. It eventually stopped just 60 centimetres below the level of the sandbags hastily built to protect the old town near the centre of Prague.

Austria, Germany and Russia

Floodwaters also soaked parts of Austria, where thousands of people fought to protect Vienna from the advancing waters of the Danube. In Germany a dam built in the southeast of the country burst, sending the waters of the River Mulde cascading towards the town of Bitterfeld. Its 16,000 inhabitants were quickly evacuated. Bridges became impassable as huge areas of the countryside were submerged under muddy brown water. Russia was one of the hardest hit countries. Here, many tourists on the Black Sea coast were swept away by raging waters.

Floods were widespread across Europe in 2002. Volunteers in Prague sandbagged the streets to protect historic buildings.

DROUGHT

Drought can happen almost anywhere in the world from time to time. Drought is a temporary absence of rainfall. If it lasts long enough farming, industry and people may suffer from water shortages.

How bad? Droughts tend to be more severe in some areas than in others. Catastrophic droughts generally occur in areas closer to the equator and close to desert regions (see map on page 23). These droughts occur when dry desert air moves northwards, making nearby areas drier than normal.

The effects In countries with only small amounts of rainfall and high evaporation, prolonged drought can cause real problems, especially if these countries are poor. In the mid-1980s parts of Ethiopia, Sudan, Somalia and Eritrea received no rain but had scorching temperatures for months. As a result the landscape changed from one of lush green grasslands to a brown, dry desert like landscape with no pasture. Some of the land did not even recover when rain finally began to fall. Animals hooves had churned up the soil, killing the grasses and plants so that the vegetation could not grow again. These areas turned into desert.

Without tree and plant roots to hold the soil together after a drought, soil erosion is a common problem.

If a drought is prolonged, vegetation and trees will eventually die and the area will turn into desert.

Surviving drought In some countries people have to walk long distances to collect water during droughts, particularly if they have animals to look after.

Other countries, such as Egypt, have found new water sources for people to use and irrigate their land. Large irrigation schemes, run from a network of canals close to the Aswan Dam on the Nile, allow fruit, vegetables and crops to be grown in areas that were once desert.

In Saudi Arabia desalinated water from the sea is used to irrigate the land. In Sinai 'trickle irrigation' from a system of plastic pipes has turned hundreds of hectares of dry land into a huge market garden producing oranges, apricots and even roses. Good drainage in these areas is essential, otherwise the ground will become waterlogged. Standing water will evaporate and leave a build up of natural salts in which new plants will not grow.

A Masai livestock farmer in Tanzania travels to find water in an area affected by drought.

A Sri Lankan tree house, built to protect a family from elephants.

Case study: Sri Lanka

Southern Sri Lanka suffered from a partial drought between 1996 and 2002. For 22 months, throughout 2001 and much of 2002, almost no rain fell. Most of the rivers, reservoirs, ponds and wells dried up and water carried through pipes was only available for a few hours each day. Fresh water had to be supplied to thousands of people in the worst affected areas.

Effect on the landscape
The tropical landscape changed from being lush and green to dry and grey. In some small villages families had to sleep in tree houses as they were fearful of being attacked and trampled on by elephants as they came into villages looking for food and water.

Drought ends
A return to 'normal' weather brought the drought to an end in the final months of 2002. The following year saw plenty of rain and a record-breaking rice crop. Some areas even suffered from flooding.

HURRICANES AND TORNADOES

Hurricanes and tornadoes are violent weather phenomena that can have sudden and devastating effects on the Earth.

A hurricane as seen from space.

Hurricanes
Hurricanes are violent whirling storms, which can be up to 500 kilometres wide. Winds circulate around them at speeds of over 120 kilometres per hour. They begin over warm oceans in areas of low pressure. The air swirls around the low pressure centre and the winds get stronger. Near the central 'eye', wind speeds of up to 300 kilometres per hour can occur.

Hurricanes are called 'typhoons' when they occur in the western Pacific Ocean, 'cyclones' over the Indian Ocean, and 'willy willies' in Australia. About six to eight tropical storms each year reach hurricane status.

A banana plantation in Honduras detroyed by Hurricane 'Mitch' in 1998.

Follow it through: hurricane development

Tropical wind near West Africa

It moves west, gathers strength by the energy released from water vapour over the ocean, and becomes a tropical storm

Storm surge

As a hurricane moves towards the coast, the wind and rain combine with the force of the sea to produce a huge tide called a 'storm surge', which can often reach several metres above normal sea level.

High winds and torrential rain – two billion tonnes of which may fall in a day – combined with the storm surge, cause flooding and damage to coasts. Trees are uprooted, houses are wrecked and communications are disrupted. Once over land, however, hurricanes cannot continue to draw their power from the warm ocean and so will eventually die out.

Tornadoes

Tornadoes, or 'twisters' as they are sometimes called, are the most violent weather systems known on Earth. These violent spinning funnels of air develop in turbulent storm clouds between quickly rising and falling air. They normally develop towards the end of a hot day. The winds of a tornado can reach speeds of over 300 kilometres per hour but they may measure only a few hundred metres in diameter and last for only a few minutes.

Building wreckers

The most severe tornadoes occur in the Mid-west of the USA in the late spring and early summer. Here, some 700 are reported each year. They rip through the landscape, making a noise like an express train, destroying virtually everything in their path. Because of the differences in air pressure, buildings they pass through appear to explode and cars, animals and people are whisked into the air often landing kilometres away.

Tornadoes are dramatic, and terrifying, sights.

Case study: Hurricane Floyd

Hurricane Floyd started out as a tropical wave, an area of curved cloud, near the Cape Verde Islands in the Atlantic Ocean close to West Africa on 2nd September 1999. It surged through several US states and Canada before finally dying out in the North Atlantic Ocean on 19th September.

Destruction

Floyd's visit cost the lives of 74 people and caused over $6 billion in damage. About 7,000 homes were destroyed, 17,000 were made uninhabitable, and 56,000 damaged. Most crops in its path were ruined, roads were washed out, thousands of trees were uprooted, and landslides were set off.

Floods spread across North Carolina inundating fields, roads and houses. Many people spent several days on their rooftops waiting to be rescued.

| As more energy is released, winds increase to hurricane strength | Over land, winds cause severe damage | Winds begin to lessen over land where there is no more energy from evaporating water | Hurricane dies out |

EL NIÑO

Some experts believe that heavy rainfall in Indonesia is caused by El Niño.

El Niño is a regularly occurring phenomenon which is believed to affect the weather across much of the planet. It has been linked with droughts in southern and eastern Africa and Asia, as well as unusual weather in parts of the USA, which caused floods and mudslides.

What is it? El Niño is a huge area of warm water, which usually lasts for about four years off the coast of South America. It then slowly crosses the Pacific, where it stays for another four years. Unusually cold ocean currents that occur when El Niño is not present are called 'La Nina'.

Scientists believe that El Niños and La Ninas have occurred for about the last 15,000 years, but the phenomenon was only discovered in the 1970s. The 10°C temperature difference in the temperature between El Niño and La Nina affects the temperature of the whole Pacific Ocean and weather systems across much of the Earth.

Follow it through:
El Niño and La Nina

West Pacific El Niño

East Pacific La Nina

Rise in sea temperatures

Fall in sea temperatures

What happens?

When warm water is near Indonesia, the air above is warmed and rises, clouds develop and the area receives heavy rainfall. On the other side of the Pacific the water is cool, the air above cannot hold much water and so dry conditions are created. But places such as Indonesia can suffer climatic extremes with heavy rainfall being replaced by drought when the warm water moves away.

Affecting weather around the world

In 2002 El Niño is thought to have caused a tornado that ripped through central Florida, USA. Winds of up to 340 kilometres per hour destroyed over 200 buildings. At the same time other tornadoes were touching down along the Atlantic and Gulf coasts of the state. Later torrential rain fell for a month in North California where extensive flooding and mudslides caused $300 million worth of damage.

The effect of El Niño outside the USA was even more severe. Two hundred people were killed and 240,000 made homeless in storms in Peru. In Indonesia a prolonged drought made forests tinder dry and fires, fanned by high winds, burned out of control. The fires and their thick smog were responsible for the deaths of 420 people, the destruction of crops and, later on, disease and famine were caused by the destruction of local water supplies.

Dry weather brought about by El Niño may be the cause of highly-destructive forest fires.

El Niño research

A major focus of research is to predict El Niño events so that governments are better prepared to tackle these kinds of catastrophes when they happen. Governments all over the world are developing emergency procedures and stockpiling resources, such as medicines and tents, to help them deal efficiently with a whole range of El Niño related extreme weather events.

Rise in air temperatures	Build up of cloud	Heavy rain events	Flooding
Fall in air temperatures	Little cloud produced	Arid events	Drought

WHAT IS CLIMATE?

Climate is the average weather pattern a place receives over at least 30 years. Unlike weather, which can have a sudden impact, a region's climate shapes and alters the landscape over time. It gives a place its character, such as dry, sandy deserts or lush green rainforests. The climate a place has depends on its distance from the equator, distance from the sea and height above sea level.

Arctic Circle

Sun's rays

Equator

Sun's rays

Earth

Atmosphere

The equator Places closer to the equator heat up more quickly and have higher temperatures than places further north or south. This is because the Earth is curved and the Sun's rays are more concentrated over the equator where the Sun is always high in the sky and directly overhead twice a year. Over polar areas, in the far north or south, the Sun appears low in the sky in the summer months and does not appear at all in the winter.

Distance from the sea The oceans and seas have a modifying effect on the climate of places around them. The sea takes longer to heat up and cool down than the land. The air over the sea is usually similar to the temperature of the sea itself. Places close to the coast receive an 'equable' climate as sea breezes keep them cooler in the summer and milder in the winter than places inland. Places inland have a more extreme climate with hotter summers and colder winters.

Different parts of the Earth receive different amounts of light and energy from the Sun – much of which is lost as it passes through the atmosphere.

The rays that reach the Earth in northern or southern areas pass through a greater amount of atmosphere and lose more energy than the rays that reach the Earth around the equator.

Around the northern and southern areas, rays are also dispersed over a larger area and so heat the land less effectively than those near the equator.

Follow it through: inland and by the sea — Sea is more dense than the land — Sea heats and cools down more slowly than land

Altitude The Sun heats land and this in turn warms the air above it. The air at lower altitudes, where most of the Earth's land can be found, is thicker and dustier than at higher altitudes and warms up more quickly. Because the air is thinner and cleaner higher up, it is not warmed as efficiently as the air below. Hills and mountains are therefore usually colder than land lower down.

Tanzania is near the equator and has a hot climate. On Mount Kilimanjaro, however, temperatures are much lower and at the very top the land is covered in snow all year round.

Take it further

Glasgow in Scotland and Moscow in Russia are each about the same distance from the equator but have very different climates, because one is closer to the sea than the other. This affects the temperature and the amount of rainfall that they receive.

◆ Find these places in an atlas, do some research to find out the climate statistics for each one and draw climate graphs – including temperature and rainfall for each month.
◆ What do you notice about the climate of each city?

Air over the sea is cooler than air over the land in the summer Air over the sea is warmer than air over land in the winter

Places close to the coast have an equable climate Places away from the coast have an extreme climate

Different vegetation occurs

The Earth's climate is constantly changing. Throughout history there have been long periods when the climate has been cold and periods when it has been warm. These changes have a major impact on the Earth's landscape.

Ice ages

About every 100,000 years, over the last million years, the Earth's temperature has fallen by about 5°C, causing an 'ice age'. Some of these ice ages lasted for thousands of years. The most recent, 20,000 years ago, is called the 'Laurentide'. Vast areas of Arctic seawater froze and large areas of land experienced prolonged sub-zero temperatures and higher snowfalls.

Glaciers were formed by the snow and these moved under pressure of the ice above it. Mountain glaciers moved down highland slopes, removing soil and wearing away rocks. The ice at the North Pole increased in size, its mass reaching 2,000 kilometres further south than it is today

In northern latitudes the effect of the ice ages on the landscape was considerable. Huge glaciers, often hundreds of metres thick, scoured the hills and valleys removing soil and rock and dumping it several kilometres away, producing a variety of new features in the landscape.

A U-shaped valley in Norway, shaped thousands of years ago by the movement of an ice-age glacier.

Little ice ages

Small drops in temperature of two or three degrees caused shorter periods of cold weather, such as the Little Ice Age of 1500 to 1700CE. Mountain glaciers advanced and rivers regularly froze so that 'Frost Fairs' – markets and carnivals – became a feature of winter life on the River Thames in London, UK.

It is likely that ice ages will occur in the future as the Earth's climate changes. At present we are experiencing a relatively warm period.

**Follow it through:
occurence of ice ages**

A change occurs in the Earth's tilt, or change in sunspot activity

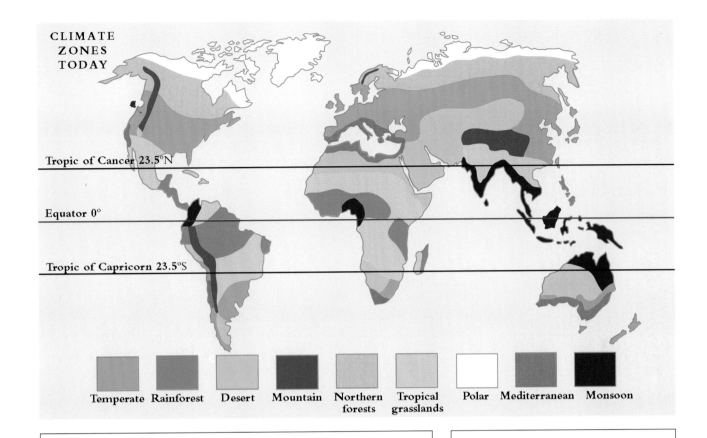

CLIMATE ZONES TODAY

Tropic of Cancer 23.5°N

Equator 0°

Tropic of Capricorn 23.5°S

Temperate | Rainforest | Desert | Mountain | Northern forests | Tropical grasslands | Polar | Mediterranean | Monsoon

Climate zones today There are nine 'climate zones' of the Earth – broad areas that have a similar climate (see map above). These areas also have similar vegetation and landscapes and are each explored further on pages 24–41.

Case study: climate in the past
The Earth's landscape itself can provide a lot of information about the climate in the past.

Geological: Glacier moraines (see page 11) often contain pollen, which gives information about the climate before and during the last ice age.
Ice: The analysis of the air trapped within ice can show the type and amount of different gases in the air at any time.
Tree rings: These can be used to see the weather over hundreds of years. Large gaps between the rings indicate wetter weather and smaller gaps drier weather.

Future climates?
Over the last 30 years, scientists have reported that the Earth is getting warmer because of the increase in 'greenhouse gases', such as carbon dioxide (see pages 42–43). They predict that the global temperature could rise by 3°C by the end of the century and this could lead to polar ice caps melting, rising sea levels submerging low land, a shifting of the world's climate patterns and more extreme weather events. In the near future, the Earth's climate zones map may look very different.

Less heat comes from the Sun ➤ Earth's temperature falls ➤ Ice age occurs

POLAR REGIONS

The polar regions in the Arctic and the Antarctic are the most northerly and southerly parts of the Earth and experience the harshest climates in the world. They have a year round average temperature of less than 10°C. Ice polished by strong winds forms most of the landscape, so the poles are inhospitable to vegetation, animal and human life.

Emperor penguins in the Antarctic huddle together during a fierce storm.

Freezing cold At the poles the Sun is never high in the sky. The temperature remains below freezing for most of the year, especially when the Sun dips below the horizon and the sky grows dark for six months (from March in Antarctica and from September in the Arctic).

The Antarctic The Antarctic is more inhospitable than the Arctic because it is a landmass and on average 2,500 metres above sea level. It is almost completely covered by a thick layer of ice and snow, some of which is over 4,700 metres deep. It is the windiest place in the world. Occasionally winds become hurricanes, which create vast areas of polished ice, worn smooth by ice crystals carried in the wind. The coldest temperature ever recorded was at Vostok in the Antarctic at –88°C.

Follow it through: polar regions

Extremely cold climate

Permanent ice forms

Ice and rain Where the ice meets the sea, large chunks sometimes break off and float away as icebergs, leaving behind enormous ice cliffs. Only about five per cent of the Antarctic is free of ice. Most of this is on the thin peninsula of land that reaches out towards South America. Underneath some of the ice lie lakes of fresh water.

Rainfall is rare and only occurs on the northern part of the Antarctica peninsula. Here some vegetation, including grass, moss and lichen, grows. Most precipitation is snow – about five centimetres a year inland and about twenty-five centimetres on the coast.

Take it further
Using resource material such as the Internet or reference books, trace an expedition to either the North or South Pole, perhaps by Shackleton, Scott or Amundsen.

◆ Look at the route they took, the landscape they crossed and the hardships they endured in order to reach the Pole.
◆ Look at how modern technology has made polar exploration easier than it was for explorers long ago.

An Antarctic iceberg breaking off from the Ross Ice Shelf.

The Arctic The Arctic, at the North Pole, is slightly warmer than the Antarctic, but still bitterly cold. It lies in a sea of permanent ice, touching land only in Greenland and the islands of northern Canada. The thinner ice over the ground around the edge of the Arctic melts during the short summer but a few centimetres below the ground remains permanently frozen. This 'permafrost' does not allow melt water to soak away and so only a few plants, moss, lichens and some grasses can grow.

The human landscape Life at the poles is difficult for people. In the Antarctic there are no permanent settlements because of the climate and the lack of minerals and fossil fuels in the region. Here there are only temporary communities of scientists, working in isolated research stations.

The Arctic does have its own native people, the 'Inuit', who traditionally were hunters eating animal meat and using their fur for clothing. In recent times many have left their homelands to live in the towns of northern Canada. Of those that remain, only a few still hunt animals for their furs.

The ground is permanently frozen → Melt water cannot escape → Little vegetation can grow

Siberian taiga, north of Verkhoyansk.

TAIGA (NORTHERN FORESTS)

The forests of the taiga stretch in a near continuous belt of coniferous trees across northern parts of America, Scandinavia and Siberian Russia, and border the Arctic regions. (There are no true areas of taiga in the southern hemisphere.) These areas have long severe winters, often with six months below freezing, and short summers. During the late spring and summer the landscape is transformed – grasses, wild plants and shrubs add to the greenery of the forests.

Temperature extremes The lowest ever recorded temperature (-68°C) outside of the Arctic was recorded at Verkhoyansk in the Siberian taiga. The clear winter skies and cold winds from the Arctic cause temperatures to fall to very low levels and so the tree covered landscape is covered with ice and snow from late autumn to early spring.

Because places far away from the sea experience a wide range of temperatures Verkhoyansk can get quite hot in the summer months. The hottest recorded temperature here was 36°C.

**Follow it through:
northern forests**

Long cold winters

Short growing season

Trees This heavily glaciated landscape of hills and valleys is largely covered by extensive forests of larch, pine and spruce, with bogs occurring in poorly drained hollows left by glaciers. The trees are suited for survival in these inhospitable lands of extremes. They are conical in shape so they shed snow quickly, preventing the loss of branches, and they have needle leaves, often with waxy coatings, to prevent water loss and provide protection from the harsh dry winds. They are evergreen so they can begin to make food as soon as it is warm enough in spring, and dark in colour to help them absorb as much heat as possible.

Autumn in the Denali National Park, Alaska, USA.

Take it further

In Alaska and Siberia, oil and gas fields have been developed to help supply the USA and Russia. Pipelines run overground in the north of Alaska and to Valdez in the south. Service roads have been built next to them to provide easy access, should they need to be repaired. An underground gas pipeline links Urengoi in central Russia with Germany towards the southwest.

◆ Use an atlas to work out how long each pipeline is and, looking at the landscape, suggest a route that each might follow.

Human life Life in the sparsely populated taiga is difficult. At –25°C diesel oil freezes and at about –35°C human skin sticks to metal. People's homes in the established mining and fur trading centres are built with the harsh winter climate in mind. Houses have timber frames and are raised off the ground to prevent the warmth of the house melting the permafrost and subsiding, and also so that the doorways can be cleared of snow. Houses usually have several layers of glass in their windows to help keep out the cold.

Coniferous trees suited to environment

Conical in shape to shed snow
Needle leaves to reduce loss of water
Evergreen so they make food as soon as possible

Northern forests

MOUNTAINS

Mountains are distributed around the world. Most mountains occur in chains or ranges that can run for hundreds or even thousands of kilometres. Their climate depends on altitude and aspect – the direction the Sun is in. The climate of mountains is unique as it changes dramatically within a few hundred metres. Higher mountains have permanent snow on their summits while their lower slopes will share the same climate as the land the mountain is situated in.

At the top It is always cold on the top of mountains as the temperature falls by about 1°C for every 100 metres ascended and so the climate will be very different to that experienced lower down.

Towards the summit of the highest mountains a layer of snow can be found that may have accumulated over hundreds of years. This will slowly change to ice and form a glacier that will eventually move downhill, forced by gravity and the weight of snow and ice above it.

As the glacier moves it wears away the valley floors below creating a variety of landscape features such as U-shaped valleys (see page 11) and hanging valleys with waterfalls. Hanging valleys are formed when the main valley and the valleys that enter it (tributary valleys) are eroded at different rates. The floors of the tributary valleys are deepened at a slower rate so the difference between the depths of the two valleys increases over time. The tributaries are left high above the main valley with their streams falling, sometimes almost vertically, into the larger valley below.

Autumn foliage at the bottom of this mountain in Colorado, USA, contrasts with the snow at the top.

Lower slopes On the lower slopes broadleaf trees can sometimes grow, while higher up conifers survive until the climate becomes too cold for them. At this point, slow growing alpine plants and grasses will be found. Higher still, where the climate is harsh, nothing will grow as the mountain slopes are composed of bare rock.

Case study: Chamonix, France

Chamonix is a French ski resort located about 80 kilometres southeast of the city of Geneva in Switzerland. It is at the foot of Mont Blanc, which is the highest mountain in the Alps at 4,810 metres.

Tourist attraction

Chamonix attracts visitors at all times of the year. In the summer people enjoy activities such as mountain biking and hiking. It is also a very popular winter ski resort. It has some of the longest ski runs in the Alps (170 kilometres) including some on glaciers.

Mountain changes

The town grew, like many others in the area, from a small village to a large modern resort. But tourism in this environment is a mixed blessing. On the one hand tourists bring jobs to people who traditionally relied on sheep farming on the poor mountain soils. But delicate slow growing mountain plants were being destroyed by walkers and skiers. Walkers also exposed soil on footpaths, which with heavy rain were eroded. Soon Chamonix and other resorts in this area became the target for environmental protection groups. As a result virtually no new ski resorts have been built in this part of the Alps for over 20 years. Instead efforts now go into improving the resorts already there.

Take it further

Look at the summer and winter holiday brochures for a holiday resort in the Alps.

- ◆ Choose a destination and hotel.
- ◆ Describe the landscape it is in and find out what you can about the weather it receives in the winter and in the summer.

Skiers walk up 'Vallée Blanche' in Chamonix, France. Constant use changes the landscape of the mountains.

TEMPERATE REGIONS

Temperate climates are those that do not have extremes of temperature or rainfall over the year and include most of Europe, New Zealand, East Asia, parts of Chile and the north of the USA.

Inland or coastal There are differences in the climates of temperate regions. Those close to the sea have a 'maritime' climate, where there is little difference in the winter and summer temperatures. Those further inland have a 'continental' climate, with warmer summers and colder winters. Places on the same latitude therefore can have noticeably different climates (see pages 20–21).

The Gulf Stream, a warm ocean current coming north and east across the Atlantic Ocean from the Gulf of Mexico, helps to keep places in Western Europe cooler in the summer and warmer in the winter than places inland and away from its influence. For example Montreal in Canada has an average January temperature of -6°C and an average July temperature of 26°C, a range of 32 degrees. In Bordeaux, in western France, temperatures of 6°C and 21°C are usual for the same months, a range of 15 degrees. Both these places lie on the same latitude.

Farming Temperate regions experience the types of weather needed for successful farming, including mild to warm temperatures, rainfall all the year round and many hours of sunshine. This

Follow it through: temperate regions

Gentle climate

Good soil and weather for farming

has meant that the landscape in temperate areas has been more dramatically altered by people, than many other areas.

Most of the natural vegetation of the temperate zones, such as broad-leafed trees (oak, elm and ash) have been cleared for farming. In some parts of Canada and the USA, for example, this has completely altered the landscape.

People places Although temperate regions cover only about eight per cent of the Earth's surface they are home to about 40 per cent of the world's population. This is due to the equable climate: neither too hot in the summer months nor too cold during the winter, which makes living in the regions easier and more comfortable.

An increasing proportion of people living in temperate regions live in urban areas. This puts pressure on resources and the surrounding natural landscape. More land is needed for housing, industry and transport and to provide landfill sites. New sources of water have to be found or supplies brought in from other areas. These need to be stored, cleaned and purified in reservoirs and treatment works.

Much of the land in temperate regions is used for farming.

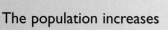

The population increases

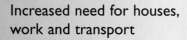

Increased need for houses, work and transport

Pressure on the land

MEDITERRANEAN CLIMATE

The Mediterranean climate can be found in parts of the world between 30 and 50 degrees north and south of the equator, in central and southern California, central Chile, southern Australia, the Cape area of South Africa and lands that border the Mediterranean Sea. Mediterranean climates experience long hot summers and mild winters.

Warm and dry
In Mediterranean climates temperatures rarely drop below 5°C in the winter while the average summer temperature reaches 27°C. Rainfall is fairly low, ranging between 280 and 600 millimetres a year. Frosts are rare but when they do occur they can cause great damage to the delicate crops that grow there.

The natural landscape of the Mediterranean regions is one of thick-barked coniferous trees, stunted evergreen oak, and sparse shrubs and grasses.

Farming
Land around the Mediterranean is generally intensively cultivated as good farming land is fairly scarce. In many places, soils are poor and the land is rocky and so small areas of better land are not wasted. Even areas of only a few square metres may be planted with vegetable or salad crops.

Terraced fields, cut like steps into the sides of hills, are a common sight as these conserve water from the limited rainfall. In the more fertile and larger fields in the valley floors, olives, grapes, citrus fruits and wheat are grown. Because of the summer drought and high temperatures most of these crops are irrigated to enable them to survive and ripen.

The natural landscape of these areas has, in many places, been altered by farmers, who have removed scrub and grasses for their crops.

A grove of irrigated orange trees in the Algarve, Portugal.

Wind damage

Strong winds can sometimes cause considerable damage to crops, especially vines. Some Mediterranean countries suffer from the 'Sirocco' (see page 7), a hot dry wind that blows dust across the sea from the Sahara Desert in the south.

The 'mistral' blows cold air north to south along the Rhone Valley in France, which acts as a wind tunnel for the strong, often hurricane-force, gusts. Again, this can cause great damage to newly planted crops.

The 'Santa Ana' wind blows hot dry air from the deserts of California, and other nearby states, causing damage to crops and bringing dust into the cities of the western coast. It also fans the flames of forest fires and can lead to the devastation of thousands of hectares of natural woodland.

Holiday destination

The lands bordering the Mediterranean Sea have been an attractive destination to many people in Europe seeking a cheap holiday in almost guaranteed summer sunshine, ever since affordable package holidays became available in the 1970s. But, this has had a dramatic effect on these countries, particularly places on the coasts. Thousands of hotels and tourist attractions have sprung up, causing many changes to the areas.

Benidorm on the Costa Blanca of Spain has been changed dramatically by the influx of tourists attracted to its Mediterranean climate.

TROPICAL GRASSLANDS (SAVANNA)

The tropical grasslands or savannas are located between 10 and 20 degrees north and south of the equator and include; parts of India and west Africa, northern Australia and parts of South America, such as the 'cerrado' of Brazil. Rain falls for most of the year but there is a dry season. Temperatures average 25-30°C all year round. The landscape consists of a vast area of grassland punctuated with occasional drought-resistant trees and shrubs.

Wet and dry seasons The climate of the savanna has distinct wet and dry seasons with most rainfall occurring in the summer months.

During the dry season temperatures may be around 20-22°C rising to 25-30°C just before the rains arrive. At this time the grass is brown and dry and almost completely lacking in nutrients, while the soil is baked hard. Most rain falls in the form of thunderstorms with torrential rain over the course of just a few weeks. Up to a metre of rain can fall in this time.

Much of this rainfall collects in hollows to form shallow lakes and pools, as the rain cannot easily soak through the hard baked ground. The rain transforms the landscape: dry grasses and plants quickly put on lush new growth and dormant seeds burst into life.

A storm gathers over the savanna in the Masai Mara, Kenya.

Follow it through: Serengeti changes

South of region is lush and green, animals graze

Rains move north

A kopje, or small hill, in the Serengeti National Park, Tanzania.

The Serengeti National Park is one of the most famous wildlife sanctuaries in the world. 'Serengeti' is a Masai word meaning 'endless plains' – appropriate as this part of the savanna covers an area of 14,763 square kilometres. It is home to over three million large mammals that roam the plains in total freedom.

The grasslands are broken up by 'kopjes' (pronounced copy) – rounded granite rock outcrops which are the result of cracking and erosion from exposure to the Sun, wind and rain. There are patches of acacia, broad-topped drought-resistant woodland, swamps and lakes that fill and empty with the passing of the seasons.

The Serengeti changes with the passing rain. In May in southern Tanzania the grasses start to disappear and the giant herds move north following the storm clouds to fresh grazing in the north. By November these grasses are exhausted and the herds return to the south where the whole cycle begins again.

Game reserves   Game reserves, including the Serengeti in Tanzania and the Masai Mara in Kenya as well as those in Botswana, Zimbabwe and South Africa, are most closely associated with the landscape of the savanna. Throughout these areas there is a continuous cover of grasses, often well over a metre tall. Trees are sparse in this semi-arid landscape, only growing where there are cracks in the brick hard ground or where there is deep soil. The acacia tree is found in East Africa as well as thorn bushes, palms and some fruit trees which provide food and shade for a wide variety of animals and birds.

In the south vegetation dies out

North becomes lush → Animals move north → The grasses in the north are exhausted → Animals move south to new pastures, following the rain again

DESERTS

Desert landscapes are found throughout the world. They occur in areas where the rainfall is less than 250 millimetres a year. In hot deserts, where evaporation is high, hardly any vegetation will be able to survive. In some deserts years can pass with no rainfall at all: parts of the Atacama Desert in Chile are said to have had no rainfall for over a hundred years.

Hot deserts
Hot deserts occur mainly between 15 and 30 degrees north and south of the equator. Deserts cover about 14 per cent of the surface of the Earth. The Sahara is the largest desert in the world with an area slightly greater than the USA.

Hot deserts experience extremely high temperatures during the day, often close to 50°C and low temperatures during the night, as there is usually no cloud to stop the daytime heat from escaping.

Cold deserts
Not all deserts are hot – the Gobi Desert is a cold desert. It lacks rain because the winds that cross the desert are dry, any rain that they are carrying having fallen near coastal areas. Winters are cold and although summers are warm they are short and little rain falls.

Monument valley, Navajo Tribal Park, Utah, USA.

Striking formations
Because of the harsh climate, desert landscapes are unique and striking. As there is virtually no vegetation the actual colours of the land can be seen. Rocky deserts may be punctuated with 'inselbergs' or 'island mountains' of harder more resistant rock and flat-topped hills called 'mesas' and 'buttes' which are found in the North American deserts.

Follow it through: desertification

Farmers need land for grazing animals

Trees are removed

Some parts of the Sahara are criss-crossed with 'wadis' – dry steep-sided river valleys that can quickly fill with water after a storm, and then just as quickly empty and dry up.

In sandy deserts features are produced by the wind blowing sand into crescent-shaped dunes called 'barchans' or long thin 'seif dunes' which move slowly in the direction of the prevailing wind.

Dust storms are common in deserts. They occur quickly and are hot and abrasive, preventing people from travelling or even going outside.

After spring rains, Californian poppies burst into life in the Mojave Desert, California, USA.

Plants   Plants in the desert tend to be ground hugging shrubs and stumpy trees with small thick leaves to help conserve water. The seeds of some plants lie on the ground, often for years, waiting for the rain to come. When it does, they grow and flower quickly so transforming the hostile landscape into a carpet of colour.

Desertification   People have played a major part in increasing the size of many deserts by removing trees and allowing their animals to overgraze the sparse vegetation. Trees not only help to bind the poor soils together but also increase the amount of water vapour in the air.

Creating desert from semi-arid regions bordering deserts in this way is called desertification. This is happening in the Sahel region which borders the Sahara Desert in Africa. When an area changes to desert it is difficult to return it to its previous state although irrigation and afforestation, tree-planting schemes, have had some success.

Tree roots no longer hold the soil together ▶ The soil erodes ▶ Land turns to desert ▶ Farmers move on to a new area

RAINFORESTS

Tropical rainforest in St Lucia, West Indies.

The rainforest stretches in a broad belt around the middle of the Earth within 10 and 15 degrees north and south of the equator. It includes the giant river basins of the Amazon in South America and the Congo in Central Africa, Central America, Southeast Asia and northern Australia.

Rain and Sun   Rain occurs on most days, usually in the form of heavy thunderstorms, which rattle around the forest soaking the trees and the ground. Each day begins sunny and hot, the damp ground from the previous day's rain slowly evaporates and cumulus clouds begin to develop. These darken and by the late afternoon or early evening rain begins to fall leaving the nights clear and dry.

An orang-utan in rainforest in Borneo.

Follow it through: rainforest climate

Trees cleared for farming

Plant roots no longer draw up water

Plants As a result plants and trees cover the landscape. There is no winter and the temperature in the rainforest is more or less the same every day, varying only by about 2°C over the year from an average of about 28°C. Plants can therefore grow, flower and fruit at any time so that the rainforest is always lush and green.

Local climate For many years rainforests have been cleared for farming and mining. In the long-term this may have an effect on the climate of the tropics. Plant roots draw up water from the ground. Water evaporates from the surface of their leaves, turning to vapour and mixing with the air. This helps to form the clouds, and the rain falls back on the forest again. With fewer trees less water evaporates, so less falls as rain. The climate of the rainforest may change so that instead of daily rainfall there may be droughts.

Wind and rain damage When trees are removed the soil may be eroded by wind and heavy rain. This leaves only small patches of rainforest, which may not survive.

Global climate As well as altering the local climate the destruction of the rainforests may also affect the global climate, as less carbon dioxide is absorbed from the atmosphere and less oxygen is returned to it (see page 42).

The destruction of the rainforest for farming, mining and roads threatens rainforest climates.

Less water evaporates into the atmosphere from leaves ▶ Less clouds are formed ▶ Less rain, so the vegetation changes further

MONSOON LANDS

Planting rice after monsoon rains in Malaysia.

Monsoon climates can be found in India, Bangladesh and Southwest Asia and in the tropical regions of West Africa, northern Australia and western Columbia. The term 'monsoon' was used by Arab sailors to describe the shifting winds that blow over the Indian Ocean and the Arabian Sea. In parts of India the monsoon can be very dramatic: some places may receive three-quarters of their annual rainfall in just three months.

Good farming land The landscape of areas in monsoon climates is one of tropical evergreen trees interspersed with occasional grasslands, much of which is farmed. Large amounts of rice are cultivated in these regions and farmers rely on the cycle of the monsoon and the rains that it brings to produce a good crop of rice.

The monsoon rain can also be destructive for farming, however. The soil can easily be washed away by the heavy rain, so farmers have to take measures to protect it, such as terracing and building earth banks to prevent run-off.

Follow it through: monsoon

Stable air covers the Indian sub-continent

Sun heats the land, temperatures rise

Case study: the Indian monsoon

In March and April the heat in India begins to build so that by May some of the highest temperatures of the year occur. As the land heats up there is an ever-increasing difference between the temperature of the land and the temperature of the sea. The mass of hot air over the land rises and cooler moist air from over the sea is drawn in to take its place. The land warms this air and it rises quickly and then cools and condenses causing droplets of water to merge and form raindrops which eventually fall to the ground as torrential rain.

Himalaya region

The south and west of India receive most of the country's monsoon rainfall. Here the monsoon is more dramatic than anywhere else in the world, as the mountains of the Himalayas and the Hindu Kush trap the moisture over the sub-continent, so allowing the monsoon to continue for several months.

Disasters

With a population of about one billion people a failure of the monsoon can ruin harvests and cause widespread famine as crops wither in parched fields. Too much rain, however, may bring catastrophic flooding causing thousands of people to lose their lives as huge expanses of fertile, productive land are covered in an enormous floodwater lake.

A dark stormy sky at the arrival of the Indian monsoon.

Strong winds blow inshore from the southwest

Storm clouds develop

Monsoon occurs

THE FUTURE

Changes in the heat produced by the Sun cause climate to change naturally, but over the last 30 years many scientists have reported that the Earth is getting warmer due to the increase in 'greenhouse gases'. They are concerned that this will cause changes to the world's weather and even eventually change our climate.

What is global warming?

Greenhouse gases are carbon dioxide, nitrous oxide and methane. These are produced by human activity – burning fossil fuels such as coal, the fumes from car exhausts and the spread of intensive agriculture are the main causes. The gases combine to reduce the amount of heat escaping from the Earth's surface and cause it to become warmer.

Another problem is deforestation. Trees absorb carbon dioxide and release oxygen and so deforestation across vast areas of the world, especially in the rainforests, has reduced the Earth's ability to remove the excess carbon dioxide in the atmosphere.

Pollution from industry is thought to be one of the causes of global warming.

Follow it through: global warming

Destruction of forests
Increased use of fossil fuel
Increased use of cars

Increase in greenhouse gases

What is the effect?
Although virtually all scientists agree that the Earth is getting warmer, they disagree on how much the temperature will rise and what the effects of this might be. The most reliable predictions say that a 3°C rise is likely before the end of this century.

As the temperature of the Earth rises they suggest that the ice caps over the North and South Poles will melt, sea levels will rise and there will be an increase in extreme weather events. Low-lying coastal areas will come under threat from the sea, especially during storm surges, and some islands will disappear. The amount of rainfall the Earth receives is expected to increase overall, especially in Central Africa and high northern latitudes. However in some places, such as southern Europe, southern Africa, Australia and Central America, rainfall will decrease.

Global warming may, over time, alter the size and distribution of many of the Earth's climatic zones. For example, there may be new areas of desert, existing desert areas may receive more rainfall and temperate regions may become more Mediterranean in character, with higher summer and winter temperatures.

What is being done?
In 1997, at the Kyoto Climate Summit, more than 1,500 scientists called on the world's governments to take action to reduce levels of human-induced global warming and to show a new commitment to protecting the global environment.

Despite scientists' concerns, governments of some countries are reluctant to enforce a reduction of greenhouse gas emissions because they fear that it will make products more expensive, put people out of work and harm their economies.

Take it further
Find out what you can about greenhouse gases, how they are caused and the effect they have on the Earth's climate.

◆ Make an information leaflet outlining the facts, your concerns and suggestions as to how to create a better future for everyone.

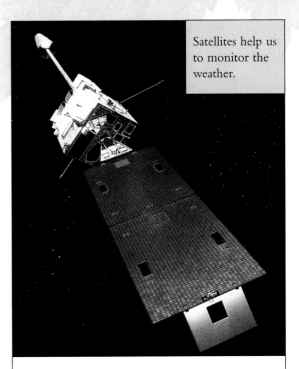

Satellites help us to monitor the weather.

Forecasting
Inventions such as weather satellites will help us keep track of any changes to global weather patterns. These monitor snow and ice cover, as well as sea surface temperature and tell us what is happening to our world. We have the technology and the ability to slowly change our climate; the question is, how much do we really want to?

| Increase in temperature | Melting ice caps, rises in sea levels | More extreme weather events |

GLOSSARY

Acid rain Rain that contains sulphuric and nitric acid which over time may damage vegetation and life in streams and lakes.

Afforestation Large scale tree-planting.

Air pressure The weight of the atmosphere pressing on the Earth's surface.

Atmosphere A blanket of air about 100 kilometres thick that encircles the Earth.

Cloud A dense mass of water droplets and/or ice crystals visible in the sky.

Drought A long continuous period of dry weather.

Glacier A slow-moving river of ice.

Equator An imaginary line running east and west around the centre of the Earth.

Gorge A narrow steep-sided river valley.

Humidity The amount of water vapour held in the air.

Hurricane An intense spinning storm with violent winds and torrential rain.

Iceberg A mass of ice that has broken away from an ice sheet.

Ice cap A permanent covering of ice – such as at the poles.

Ice age A time in Earth's history when thick ice sheets covered much of the mid-latitudes (40–60 degrees) in the northern hemisphere.

Irrigation Taking water to dry land through channels, sprinklers and hoses.

Landscape The face of the Earth.

Latitude Imaginary circles drawn around the Earth in an east–west direction.

Longitude Imaginary circles drawn around the Earth in a north–south direction.

Meander A winding curve in the course of a river.

Mountain A mass of land over 300 metres high.

Ozone (layer) A form of oxygen, which comprises a layer from 15–50 kilometres above the Earth's surface.

Pole One of the two ends (the North Pole and the South Pole) of the imaginary axis on which the Earth turns. On most maps they are shown at the top and bottom.